DUDLEY SCHOOLS
LIBRARY SERVICE

KU-213-122

Schools Library and Information Services

S00000725473

Spot the Difference

Eyes

Daniel Nunn

HEINEMANN
LIBRARY

www.heinemann.co.uk/library
Visit our website to find out more information about **Heinemann Library** books.

To order:
☎ Phone 44 (0) 1865 888066
▤ Send a fax to 44 (0) 1865 314091
▢ Visit the Heinemann Bookshop at www.heinemann.co.uk/library to browse our catalogue and order online.

First published in Great Britain by Heinemann Library, Halley Court, Jordan Hill, Oxford OX2 8EJ, part of Harcourt Education. Heinemann is a registered trademark of Harcourt Education Ltd.

© Harcourt Education Ltd 2007.
The moral right of the proprietor has been asserted.

All rights reserved. No part of this publication may be reproduced, stored in a retrieval system, or transmitted in any form or by any means, electronic, mechanical, photocopying, recording, or otherwise, without either the prior written permission of the publishers or a licence permitting restricted copying in the United Kingdom issued by the Copyright Licensing Agency Ltd, 90 Tottenham Court Road, London W1T 4LP (www.cla.co.uk).

Editorial: Tracey Crawford, Cassie Mayer, Dan Nunn, and Sarah Chappelow
Design: Jo Hinton-Malivoire
Picture Research: Erica Newbery
Production: Duncan Gilbert

Originated by RMW
Printed and bound in China by South China Printing Company

10 digit ISBN 0 431 18238 8
13 digit ISBN 978 0 431 18238 4

11 10 09 08 07
10 9 8 7 6 5 4 3 2 1

British Library Cataloguing in Publication Data
Nunn, Daniel
  Eyes. - (Spot the difference)
  1.Eye - Juvenile literature 2.Vision - Juvenile literature
  I.Title
  573.8'8
A full catalogue record for this book is available from the British Library.

Acknowledgements
The publishers would like to thank the following for permission to reproduce photographs: Alamy pp. **4** (Nature Picture Library), **15** (Guillen Photography), **16** (NaturePicks), **17** (Steve Bloom Images); Ardea pp. **6** (Chris Harvey), **8** (Jean Michel Labat), **12** (John Daniels), **14** (Ferrero-Labat), **19** (John Daniels); Corbis p. **21** (O'Brien Productions); FLPA p. **7** (Minden Pictures/JH Editorial/Cyril Ruoso); Getty Images p. **10** (Digital Vision); Nature Picture Library pp. **5** (Bruce Davidson), **9** (Meul/ARCO), **11** (John Downer), **13** (Phil Savoie), **18** (Georgette Douwma); Science Photo Library p. **20** (Mark Thomas).

Cover photograph of a tiger's eyes reproduced with permission of Steve Bloom.

Every effort has been made to contact copyright holders of any material reproduced in this book. Any omissions will be rectified in subsequent printings if notice is given to the publishers.

DUDLEY PUBLIC LIBRARIES
L
725473   SCH
JS91.5

Contents

What are eyes?

eye

Why do animals have eyes?

Animals use their eyes to see.

Where are animals' eyes?

Animals' eyes are on
their heads.

This is a gorilla.
It has eyes at the front of its head.

This is a zebra.
It has eyes on the
sides of its head.

This is an earthworm.
It has no eyes at all.

Different eyes

Eyes come in many shapes and sizes.

This is an owl.
It has round eyes.

This is a mole.
It has small eyes.

This is a frog. It has bulging eyes.
Can you spot the difference?

This is a leopard.
It has shiny eyes.

This is a fish.
It has bright yellow eyes.

Amazing eyes

big eye

little eye

This is a bee. It has two big eyes and three little eyes.

This is an eagle.
It can see a tiny mouse
from high up in the air.

stalk

This crab has two stalks on its head.
Its eyes are on the end of the stalks.

18

This is a chameleon.
Its eyes move separately.
Can you spot the difference?

Your eyes

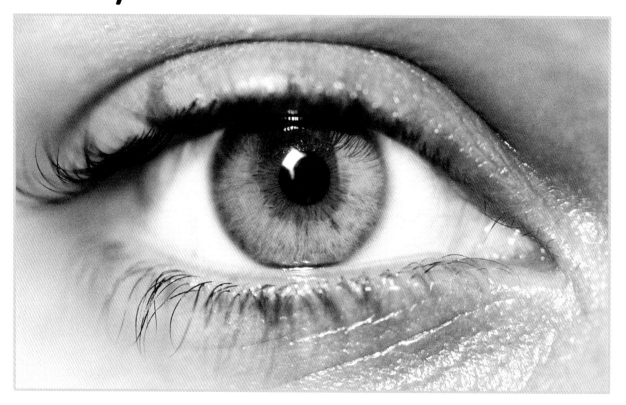

People have eyes, too. Like animals, people use their eyes to see.

What colour are your eyes?

Can you remember?

Which animal has bulging eyes?
Which animal has eyes on the side
of its head?

Picture glossary

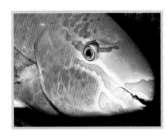

bright full of colour

bulging something that sticks out

stalk long, thin "antenna" that some crabs have on their head

Index

Notes to parents and teachers

Before reading

Talk about how we use our eyes to see. Point at things nearby and things far away and ask the child to do the same.

Ask the children to look at friends' eyes. What do they see? Talk about pupils, irises, eyelashes, and the whites of the eyes. Do they think all animals' eyes are the same?

After reading

Play "Hide the coloured wool": Hide strands of different coloured wools at different heights around the room. Give pairs of children one strand and challenge them to find as many matching strands as they can.

Play "Pin the tail on the donkey": Draw a large outline of a donkey (without a tail!) Make a paper tail. Blindfold each child in turn, spin them round once then challenge them to pin the tail on the donkey.

Titles in the *Spot the Difference* series include:

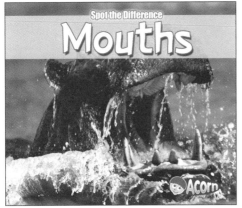

Hardback   0 431 18239 6

Hardback   0 431 18238 8

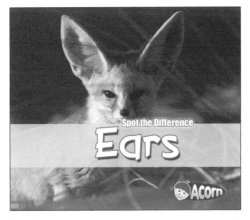

Hardback   0 431 18237 X

Hardback   0 431 18236 1

Find out about other titles from Heinemann Library on our website www.heinemann.co.uk/library